THE AEROBATS

THE AEROBATS

THE WORLD'S GREAT AERIAL DEMONSTRATION TEAMS

Bill Yenne

MALLARD PRESS

ACKNOWLEDGEMENTS

The author wishes to extend special thanks to Colonel HR Haeberli of the Swiss Air Force for making his personal files available for our use.

PICTURE CREDITS

All photographs are courtesy of the respective air forces depicted, with the following exceptions:
British Aerospace 4-5, 38, 39, 40-41, 42, 43, 44-45
John Campo 20
Harry Gann, McDonnell Douglas 9 (both), 13 (bottom)
Joe Martinez 1, 19 (top, both), 21, 22, (top), 23 (top), 26-27, 31 (bottom both), 32 (all three), 33 (bottom left), 58, 66-67, 68-69
McDonnell Douglas 14, 15, 16, 17, gatefold (inside and out)
Rockwell International 64 (bottom)
© Bill Yenne 10, 10-11, 12, 13 (top)

Page 1: **F-16 Falcons of the US Air Force Thunderbirds execute a sudden pull-out.**
Page 2-3: **Two F/A 18 Hornets of the US Navy's Blue Angels. In this maneuver, the two solo pilots—Numbers 5 and 6—approach one another, this time to demonstrate the control they have over their aircrafts' roll rate. They roll their aircraft 360 degrees, pausing after each 90 degrees of roll, and cross at center point in inverted flight as they perform the opposing four-point hesitation roll.**
These pages: **In a maneuver similar to the Blue Angels' opposing four-point hesitation roll, the RAF's Red Arrows combine a front cross roll with vertical rolls, and an opposition barrel roll/synchro.**

Designed by Bill Yenne.

First published in the United States of America in 1991
by The Mallard Press
Mallard Press and its accompanying design and logo are trademarks of BDD Promotional Book Company, Inc.

ISBN 0 7924 5503 7

Printed in Hong Kong

CONTENTS

THE REPUBLIC OF SINGAPORE AIR FORCE

THE BLACK KNIGHTS

In 1974, only nine years after the creation of the independent Republic of Singapore, the RSAF established its first all-local, national formation aerobatic team. Formed at Changi Air Base, the four-plane team was headed by Lieutenant Jimmy Lim. Officially known as the Black Knights, the team flew British-made Hawker Hunters. The Black Knight selected to perform solo aerobatics for the team's Singapore Air Force Day show was Michael Teo, who went on to serve as a brigadier general and squadron commander in the RSAF.

A second Black Knights team was formed for Singapore Air Force Day in 1977 at Changi AB. Led by Captain Frank Singam, who had been part of the original Black Knights, this team also used Hawker Hunters.

The Black Knight personnel reappeared in 1983, but in the meantime, another team, called the Flying Tigers, was established to perform for the 1981 Singapore Air Force Day celebrations. Commanded by Major Mark Wong, the Flying Tigers flew American-built Northrop F-5E Tigers. When the Black Knights made their next appearance over West Coast Park for Singapore Air Force Day in 1983, they were still flying Hunters but were now led by Major Joe Kua, who had been a member of the 1977 Black Knights team.

In 1989, in anticipation of the Asian Aerospace 1990 Exposition, a fourth edition of the Black Knights was drawn from the RSAF's 143 Squadron, which had been cited as the nation's top fighter squadron. Commanded by Major Teo Shi On, who had flown with the Flying Tigers nearly a decade before, the 1990 Black Knights were a six-plane team, the first in RSAF history. Teo's team was equipped with American McDonnell Douglas A-4SU Super Skyhawks, the most advanced aircraft in the RSAF inventory and similar to the A-4 Skyhawk and A-4F Skyhawk II aircraft used by the US Navy's Blue Angels aerobatic team from 1974 to 1986.

During the February 1990 display, the Black Knights performed roll back, twinkle roll and 360-degree roll maneuvers among others, and closed their program with a spectacular bomb-burst maneuver of a type that is popular with many other teams.

Below and opposite: **The Black Knights and their A-4SU Skyhawks during their 1990 Air Force Day program.**

THE UNITED STATES NAVY
THE BLUE ANGELS

The oldest existing military aerobatic team in the world, the US Navy's Blue Angels gave their first demonstration at an airshow in Jacksonville, Florida on 15 June 1946 under the name 'US Navy Flight Demonstration Team.' The team was organized at the direction of the Chief of Naval Operations by Lieutenant Commander Roy 'Butch' Voris, and consisted of five World War II combat veterans flying Grumman F6F-5 Hellcats.

The first display at Jacksonville included four Hellcats in a series of aerial military maneuvers flown in close formation by the veteran combat pilots. The show climaxed with a simulated shooting down of a North American SNJ Texan training aircraft painted as a Japanese Zero. This maneuver, which delighted the crowd, was later dropped from the routine, but the tight diamond formation flown by the original pilots became a trademark of the Blue Angels.

Although the Blue Angels have existed continuously since that time (except for parts of two seasons during the Korean War), organized aerobatics within the US Navy actually date back to 1928, when the Three Sea Hawks were organized within Squadron VB-2B at North Island NAS near San Diego, California. Flying Boeing F2B-2s, the Three Sea Hawks performed at shows all over the West Coast for nearly two years. In 1929, another team, the High Hatters, was formed aboard the USS *Saratoga* by Squadron VF- 1B. The High Hatters performed for several years, until the fleet was reorganized in the 1930s.

The Three Flying Fish was formed in April 1930 around the Tactical Section of the Naval Flight Test Group at Anacostia NAS in the District of Columbia. Flying Curtiss F6C-4 aircraft, the team made, among others, an appear-

Below, from top: **An artist's conception of the Blue Angels' aircraft: the Hellcat (1946), the Bearcat (1946-49), the Panther (1949-54), the Cougar (1955-57), the Tiger (1957-68), the Phantom II (1969-73), the Skyhawk (1974-1985) and the Hornet (1986-).** *Opposite top:* **Skyhawks in a vertical climb.** *Opposite bottom:* **The view from the slot (#4) position.**

ance in 1930 at the Cleveland Air Races, but was disbanded after only one year. Another F6C-4 team was the Three Gallant L's, which existed at the same time as the Three Flying Fish. Founded by Training Squadron VN-5, this group was born at Pensacola NAS in Florida, the current home of the Blue Angels.

Several informal, unnamed Navy teams also performed during the 1930s, and even after the establishment of the Blue Angels, there were other teams in existence. There was, for example a team called the Gray Angels, so named because the three pilots were all rear admirals, and hence older than most of the Navy's pilots. The Gray Angels were established in 1948 for the purpose of showing off the Navy's first jet fighter, the McDonnell FH-1 Phantom, and not as a permanent team. After the team's first show at Idylwild Airport (now JFK International) in New York City on 31 July, public response kept the team on the airshow circuit through the end of the year.

The US Marine Corps, technically a separate operating unit of the US Navy, had several teams of its own, notably the Marine Phantoms, formed by Squadron VMG-122 at MCAS Cherry Point in North Carolina in 1949. Flying McDonnell FH-1 Phantoms, the Marine Phantoms appeared at numerous events in 1949 and 1950, but were disbanded on the eve of the Korean War. Since 1957, however, Marine Corps pilots have been represented among the men chosen as members of the Blue Angels.

Meanwhile, the F6F-5 Hellcat group, originally known only as the 'US Navy Flight Demonstration Team,' adopted the name Blue Angels in August 1946, two months after their inception as the Lancers. At this time, the team also made the transition to the newer, faster and more agile

Grumman F8F Bearcat. The prop-driven Bearcats served the team through 300 performances, until the transition to jets in 1949. The Grumman F9F-2 Panther was painted bright blue with gold lettering, with the leading edge of the wings highly polished metal. This jet was flown by the team until June of 1950, at the outbreak of the Korean War.

When the war started, the Blue Angels were ordered to serve in combat aboard the aircraft carrier USS *Princeton* as the nucleus of Fighter Squadron VF-191 (*Satan's Kittens*). It was while flying with *Satan's Kittens* that Lieutenant Commander Johnny Magda, squadron Commanding Officer, was shot down by communist MiGs in March 1951, becoming the first Blue Angel to lose his life in combat.

Late in 1951, the Chief of Naval Operations once again called on Butch Voris to reform the team using Grumman F9F-5 Panthers. The team was organized at Corpus Christi NAS Texas, drawing upon a pool of veteran wartime pilots and skilled maintenance personnel to staff the group. The first demonstration by the newly reformed Blue Angels came in May 1952 at Memphis, and for a short period in the 1952 season, two soloists flew the Chance Vought F7U-1 Cutlass to supplement the four Panthers. However, they were soon replaced with Panthers to reduce the maintenance problems introduced by using dissimilar aircraft. The straight-winged F9F-5 Panther remained the standard Blue Angels aircraft for two seasons, although an all-yellow F8F Bearcat was used as a support aircraft, and F9F-6 Panthers were used briefly.

It was during the winter of 1954-55 that the team began to fly swept-winged Grumman F9F-8 Cougars and shifted their base of operations to their present location, at Pensacola NAS, Florida, the 'Cradle of Naval Aviation.'

The faster Cougar allowed the introduction of new maneuvers, such as the thrilling fleur-de-lis, to enhance the crowd-pleasing show. The team continued to be viewed by spectators through motion pictures, television and live appearance and, in mid-season 1957, moved to new supersonic Grumman F11F-1 Tigers.

Despite the difference in aircraft trim control sensitivity and power, the team made the changeover without a

schedule disruption. The Tiger served the team for 11 years and allowed a number of new maneuvers to be displayed. The four-plane diamond landing, the six-plane delta landing, the double farvel, the half-Cuban eight and the dirty-roll maneuvers drew many more spectators.

The 1000th Blue Angels display came in 1963, and by 1965 more than 75 million viewers had seen the team perform. During the same year, the team was deployed to Europe for shows in England and France, and later to the Bahamas. The team made another European tour in 1967, visiting France, Italy and Turkey, as well as Tunisia.

At the end of 1968, after 22 years in Grumman 'cats,' the Blue Angels converted to McDonnell F-4J Phantom IIs, which were the leading fighter aircraft in the Navy, and at that time engaged in combat over Vietnam. Meanwhile, the US Air Force, which was also using Phantom IIs in Vietnam, also adopted them for their Thunderbirds Flight Demonstration Team. The Phantom gave the Blue Angels the necessary power to perform the four- plane line-abreast loop, inverted fleur-de-lis, tuck-under break and echelon landings, while the two solos were able to fly the opposing dirty rolls on takeoff.

In 1970, the team included a deployment to Panama, Puerto Rico and Ecuador in its schedule, and in 1971, while celebrating its 25th anniversary, wound up the season with a six-week deployment to the Far East. Traversing the Pacific Ocean using aerial refueling, the team performed 11 flight demonstrations in Korea, Taiwan, Japan, Guam and the Philippines.

In 1973, the team flew a four-week tour through Europe, performing 14 shows in England, France, Spain, Italy, Tur-

Above: **Racing across the sky, four Blue Angels prepare for a left echelon roll.** *Top right:* **The Blue Angels begin their dramatic fleur-de-lis maneuver.** *Right:* **Blue Angel A-4s in the delta formation over the Pensacola, Florida shoreline with** *Fat Albert*, **their USMC Lockheed C-130 Hercules.**

key and Iran. This raised the total spectator count to 114,529,800 in 1744 airshows since the initial show in 1946. On 10 December 1973, an organization change was made to alter the Flight Demonstration Team to that of Flight Demonstration Squadron.

In 1974, under Commander Tony Less, the squadron switched to McDonnell Douglas A-4F Skyhawk IIs, a more economical aircraft. This was in reaction to the worldwide energy crisis, an event that saw the US Air Force abandon its F-4 Phantoms for the smaller Northrop T-38. Though smaller than the Phantom, the shorter turning radius and faster roll capabilities of the delta-wing Skyhawks soon proved their effectiveness in the aerial demonstration role. Also, a reduction in fuel and maintenance effort required to keep the Skyhawk in show condition allowed the officers and crew members to spend more time talking to young people interested in careers in the Navy. This redirection of purpose to align Blue Angel activity with Navy recruiting was one of the main reasons for reorganizing the team into a squadron.

In October 1977, 31 years after their first performance and 14 years after their 1000th, the Blue Angels gave their 2000th performance in Atlanta, Georgia. During 1982 and 1985, the squadron again executed aerial refueling while crossing the Pacific Ocean to the Hawaiian Islands for airshow demonstrations.

Above: Flying so close together that they almost appear to be one aircraft, two Blue Angels F/A-18 Hornets prepare for a crossover roll. *Right:* In the delta vertical break, the Hornets go into a spectacular vertical dive at 8000 feet.

In 1986, at the end of the Blue Angels' 40th Anniversary season, the team retired the A-4F Skyhawk–its longest-serving aircraft type–in favor of the McDonnell Douglas F/A-18 Hornet, a first-line fighter-attack aircraft which had just been adopted for service in US Navy and US Marine Corps squadrons.

While the selection of aircraft for the team is a process not taken lightly, so it is with the pilots as well. The few annual openings are highly sought after and competition for them is extremely keen. Any Navy or Marine Corps pilot may apply for assignment if he is a career-oriented volunteer who has accumulated 1500 flight hours in tactical jet aircraft. The naval aviation community is a close-knit one and frequently the applicants know each other, thus adding to the competitive spirit. From these applicants come the final group of individuals who are then encouraged to become more familiar with the Flight Demonstration Squadron, its mission and its members and their lifestyle. As well as being good pilots, applicants must be equally comfortable filling the numerous speaking engagements they will be asked to make. The final selection of two or three members each year takes place within the squadron itself, with direct cognizance and ultimate approval of the Chief of Naval Air Training.

Each aviator in the squadron spends two years as a demonstration pilot, and then returns to an operational assignment in the fleet. In this way, more naval aviators can become a part of the Blue Angel family. Even after returning to the fleet, the adage 'Once a Blue, always a Blue!' applies. This constant turnover of personnel testifies to the high quality of training given US Navy and Marine Corps pilots.

The average age of a Blue Angel is 32 years. Each pilot has served at least four years in the Navy or Marine Corps and has completed his first operational tour at sea aboard an aircraft carrier or at a land-based installation. The most opportune time in an officer's career for assignment with the Blue Angels is just after his first operational tour of duty.

The Blue Angels' season begins in the December preceding the show season, when the commander and the events coordinator attend the annual scheduling conference in Washington, DC to determine the coming year's itinerary. Normally, the Navy receives more requests for Blue Angel demonstrations than can be accommodated, so a careful review and selection of the most productive show sites is made.

Early in January, the Blue Angels relocate from Pensacola NAS to their winter training home at the Naval Air Facility in El Centro, California. The clear, sunny winter weather of the vast Imperial Valley provides ideal conditions for flight training for the next 60 to 70 days. During that time, the team devotes its total concentration to honing flying skills and maintenance expertise to a fine edge of perfection. The pilots fly twice a day, seven days a week. The flying begins at 6:00 am and ends in the early afternoon. The remainder of the day is occupied with a physical fitness program, followed by a period of relaxation in order to be totally prepared for the next day's flying.

When the flying season begins in the spring, a pattern of operation is established. The narrator and his crew chief precede the main body to each show site by one day to give a last minute check to the extensive preparations that are completed months prior to each demonstration. On the next day, the demonstration aircraft arrive and the pilots check out the show site. One day is reserved for a practice demonstration that is used to provide the three to four days of weekly flying required to maintain peak proficiency. The official demonstration normally takes place on Saturdays and Sundays. The squadron then returns to Pensacola on Sunday evening or Monday morning, with the following day set aside for rest and relaxation. The next two days are filled with administrative chores, a practice demonstration and briefings for the next show. This weekly routine lasts until late November.

A Blue Angels demonstration consists of six aircraft performing a prescribed sequence of maneuvers. The aircraft are seen in three groupings: a diamond formation of four aircraft, two solo aircraft that oppose each other along the line of flight, or with six aircraft in a delta formation. The program begins with aircraft one through four taking off simultaneously, immediately forming a diamond while only a few feet off the 'deck.' Next, the two solos take off separately, perform rolls, and then all aircraft begin the show maneuvers.

The Blue Angels' tight diamond formation has been the squadron's trademark throughout the world since 1946. With the aircraft fuselages a mere 36 inches apart with

Above and opposite: **The diamond roll is one of the Blue Angels most thrilling maneuvers. At an airspeed of 400 mph, the Hornets begin a climb and, on a signal from the leader, roll 360 degrees as if they were welded together.**

complete wing overlap, the diamond illustrates the beauty and grace that can be achieved in formation flying.

Total concentration is devoted by each pilot to maintaining the same relative position to the other three aircraft. Equal concentration is required on the constant radio chatter which accompanies each movement of the formation. Foremost, each pilot must stay mentally ahead of the sequence of events and know at all times what his relationship is to the other aircraft in the formation and to the ground below.

The two solo pilots demonstrate the high-performance capabilities of their aircraft for the airshow audience. In order to dramatically emphasize each maneuver, they oppose each other along the flight line at closing speeds of 1000 miles per hour, and attempt to establish a collision effect from the crowd's angle of vision. This effect, or 'hit,' takes place close to the exact center point of the flight line. To do this requires exact timing.

During the season, the six Blue Angels F/A-18 show aircraft (plus one alternate) are supported by the two dozen members of a support team that accompany them on their 140,000-mile itinerary aboard a US Marine Corps C-130 Hercules transport known informally as *Fat Albert*. *Fat Albert* is painted in the same distinctive colors as the demonstration aircraft.

17

FORCA AEREA BRASILEIRA
ESQUADRILHA DA FUMACA

It was in 1952 at Afonsos Air Base near Sao Paulo that the first organized aerobatic team was formed within the air force of Brazil. The team was created thanks to the efforts of six young Air Force Academy instructors who, in their free time, performed aerobatic maneuvers to show the cadets the possibilities inherent in the North American T-6 trainers that Brazil had used since World War II, and to give the cadets confidence in flying.

The team's first air show was on 14 May 1952 during a military ceremony, and one year later, one member of the team had the idea of spraying oil in the motor's exhaust tube, which created a dense, smoky trail and tracked the team's maneuvers. From this came their name, 'Esquadrilha da Fumaca,' or 'the squadron that produces smoke.'

In 1969, the T-6 trainers were replaced within the Esquadrilha da Fumaca by seven French-built Super Fouga Magister jets. Their operational characteristics—short endurance and the need of asphalt runways for operation—didn't meet the team's needs, so they returned to flying the T-6s until 1977, when they were finally deactivated due to excessive maintenance requirements and the prohibitive cost of high-octane fuel. During those 24 years, the team had performed 1260 air shows, with 106 in 1973 alone.

Having been disbanded in 1977, the Esquadrilha da Fumaca was reborn on 21 October 1982 and officially designated as the Esquadrao de Demonstracao Aérea (Air Display Squadron or EDA). The new team was equipped from the outset with Brazilian-built Embraer 312 Tucano trainers. This airplane had several advantages, such as reduced maintenance requirements and a fuel- conservative engine. It was a highly maneuverable aircraft, had a high safety level and could be operated at acceptable cost levels.

Based at Pirassununga, home of Brazil's Air Force Academy, the team in recent years has performed throughout Brazil, as well as in Chile, Paraguay, Bolivia, Portugal, Germany, Panama and Venezuela.

Top right: **Seen here in a parasol break and level flight, the Esquadrilha da Fumaca are noted for their characteristic frothing stream of white smoke.**
Right: **Since the early 1980s, the Esquadrilha da Fumaca have performed their daring maneuvers in the EMB-312 Tucano turboprop.**

AERONAUTICA MILITARE ITALIANA

FRECCE TRICOLORI

Although the Italian Air Force's Frecce Tricolori (Tri-colored Arrows) national aerobatic team was established on 1 March 1961 at Rivolto Air Base, Italy has a long history of aerobatic showmanship. In 1930, Colonel Rino Corso Fougier, considered to be the 'spiritual father' of Italian aerobatics, formed the nation's first aerobatic school at Campformido. Fougier convinced the Italian Air Staff that a military pilot had first to be a real sportsman if he were to fly his aircraft in wartime assignments with maximum efficiency and full control.

Under Fougier, aerobatic flight resulted from strict and constant daily training in air fighting and interception. At the same time, Fougier began a program of training a formation of five planes devoted solely to aerobatic flying.

During the 1930s the Italian Air Force aerobatic teams achieved widespread fame at home and abroad, traveling to both Eastern and Western Europe, as well as to South America, where they participated in international competitions. Everywhere they went, Fougier's teams were met with enthusiasm and deep admiration, both for the pilots and for their Italian-built aircraft.

Organized display aerobatics resumed in Italy after the end of World War II, during the reorganization of the Italian Air Force. In the 1950s, Italy was represented in several national and international airshows, and the Italian Air Force staff decided to appoint each year a single Italian representative team to participate in all the airshows during the year and a reserve team that would in turn become the representative team for the subsequent year.

This rotation of teams to represent Italy at airshows had actually begun informally as early as 1950 with the estab-

Below: **The Frecce Tricolori used Fiat G-91s until 1981.** *Right:* **Aermacchi MB-339As paint the colors of Italy's flag.**

lishment of the Cavallino Rampante (Rampant Horse), formed from the Fourth Aerobrigata (Wing) of the Italian Air Force, which flew de Havilland DH-100 Vampires in airshows from 1950 to 1952. The next principal Italian Air Force team was the Getti Tonanti (Thunder Jets) of the Fifth Aerobrigata, which flew American-built Republic F-84G Thunder Jets in the 1953 through 1955 airshow seasons. Also flying F-84Gs were the Tigri Bianche (White Tigers), formed from the 51st Aerobrigata in 1955 and 1956.

When the succession of teams became official in 1956, the Cavallino Rampante of the Fourth Aerobrigata returned to the fore, now flying red-nosed North American F-86E Sabre Jets. They were in turn succeeded in 1957 by the Diavoli Rossi (Red Devils) formed from the Sixth Aerobrigata and flying Republic F-84F Thunderstreaks. In 1958, the Diavoli Rossi was joined by a second team, the Lanceri Neri (Black Lancers) of the Second Aerobrigata flying their distinctive all-black F-86Es. Both of these teams were succeeded in 1959 by the reappearance of the Getti Tonanti of the Fifth Aerobrigata, now flying F-84Fs. It was the Getti Tonanti that represented the Italian Air Force in aerobatic displays held in celebration of the 1960 Rome Olympic Games in Rome. Each of these F-84Fs were marked with different color trim and trail, with the latter bearing the five-ringed Olympic emblem.

In March 1981, the Italian Air Force formed the 313th Gruppo Addestramento Aerobatico, a squadron permanently dedicated solely to aerobatic display flying, and the

Above: The Frecce Tricolori demonstrate a crossover roll within a multiplane formation. *Below, from left:* The Frecce Tricolori during tactical combat training; over Niagara Falls and beginning their stunning parasol break.

name Frecce Tricolori was officially adopted. For its first three years, the Frecce Tricolori flew F-86E Sabre Jets painted black (as were the F-86Es of the Lanceri Neri of 1958) or dark blue.

In 1964, the Frecce Tricolori adopted the Aeritalia/Fiat G-91, the first Italian-designed jet to be regularly used by an Italian Air Force aerobatic team. The G-91 continued in service until 1981, when the Frecce Tricolori made the transition to the newer (and also Italian-built) Aermacchi MB-339A.

Today the 313th Gruppo is based at Rivolto Air Base where it maintains a year-round training schedule when not involved in aerobatic displays. This involves active combat training, as well as aerobatic training, because a significant portion of the 313th's activity is reserved for the operational training in the Close Air Support and anti-helicopter roles in wartime as established by Italian Air Force staff. In particular, all personnel are trained to achieve and maintain combat readiness, and each aircraft assigned to the 313th is convertible to a combat configuration within hours.

Below and right: **The Aermacchi MB-339As of Frecce Tricolori in formation with their tricolored smoke vents streaming.**

THE FINNISH AIR FORCE/SUOMEN SOTILASAIAMIES
JASKA 4

On 20 June 1962, two years after the delivery of the first Fouga Magisters to the Finnish Air Force, the "Fouga Magister Aerobatic Team of the Air Force Academy" made its first public performance. The team was based at Kauhava and originally included nine Valmet-built Magisters, with pilots drawn from Jaska 4 (Fighter Squadron 4). The number of Magisters was reduced to four in the mid-1960s.

Twenty years after the team was formed, the British Aerospace Hawk was adopted as the standard trainer of the Finnish Air Force, and 20 June 1987 saw the debut of the "Hawk Aerobatic Team of the Air Force Academy."

Each year the group is given unofficial, or pet names, according to the first name of the leader of Jaska 4. For the time being, the leader of the group is Captain Mika Soininen. The members of the team are not full-time aerobatic pilots, but mostly experienced flight instructors, and they train and present their program in addition to their ordinary duties.

The Jaska 4 air display consists of basic aerobatic maneuvers, including loops, barrel rolls and rolls made in a box or swan-neck formation. The program undergoes some changes and is presented a few times a year. The biggest event for Jaska 4 is the Midsummer Festival at Kauhava, their home base, which takes place on the midsummer night's eve, and attracts about 15,000 onlookers annually.

These pages: Jaska 4's four-plane diamond in tight maneuvers over the Gulf of Bothnia. The Jaska 4's exciting performances draw crowds all over Finland, especially for their annual appearance at the Midsummer Festival at Kauhava.

THE ROYAL NEW ZEALAND AIR FORCE
KIWI RED

Number 75 Squadron of the RNZAF was originally created as Number 75 Squadron of the British Royal Air Force Bomber Command. Staffed by New Zealanders during World War II, the squadron was disbanded as an RAF unit after the war and permanently transferred to RNZAF in December 1946.

Since that time, the squadron has been an operationally active fighter-bomber squadron. In 1958, for example, the squadron transferred to Malaya to equip with Canberra bombers on active service in the Malayan emergency campaign. In 1970, Number 75 Squadron was re-equipped with the American-built Douglas A-4 Skyhawk. The squadron currently operates 14 Skyhawks in a variety of roles, and regularly deploys to Australia, Malaysia, Singapore and the South Pacific. The RNZAF's Skyhawk aircraft received a major avionics refit in the late 1980s and should see service well into the mid-1990s.

Today, Number 75 Squadron is the RNZAF's principle strike squadron, responsible for filling all of the tactical jet fighter roles required for the defense of New Zealand. This includes being ready to deploy anywhere in Southeast Asia or the southwestern Pacific on short notice.

The primary operational role of the squadron is maritime surface attack, often involving operations up to 400 miles from the nearest land. The patrols are carried out in close cooperation with RNZAF Orion Maritime Patrol aircraft and ships of the Royal New Zealand Navy.

Kiwi Red exists within the context of this crack unit, employing the services of six of its best pilots as well as numerous support personnel.

Over the years, various informal aerobatic teams have existed within the RNZAF, especially in the late 1940s, and Number 75 Squadron formed its first three-man, all-jet team in 1954 for the National Aero Club Pageant at Masterton. A four-man team performed for Air Force Day in 1955 supported by a solo display aircraft. The pattern of squadron teams was repeated in 1956, at the 21st Anniversary of the RNZAF in 1958, and it is here that they won high praise from the overseas visitors.

The Number 75 Squadron aerobatic team was disbanded from 1960 to 1964; then it re-emerged under the name Yellowhammers, which was derived from the squadron insignia. The Yellowhammers were disbanded in 1970, but revived briefly for Air Force Day in 1981.

On the occasion of Air Force Day in 1983, Number 75 Squadron flew a five aircraft team which featured the first display of a low level 'plugged' barrel roll, with two aircraft connected via the air refueling hose. This was a world first for an aerobatic team.

In 1986, the squadron team, now led by Wing Com-

These pages: **Members of the Royal New Zealand Air Forces Number 75 Squadron Kiwi Red aerobatic team flying the A-4K Skyhawk aircraft, which are maintained combat-ready.**

mander Frank Sharp, performed at the Royal Australian Navy's 75th Anniversary at NAS Nowra and at RMAF Kuantan, Malaysia. The squadron carried out a further display at Rarotonga during the New Zealand Joint Services Exercise in the Cook Islands.

In January 1987, the squadron formed a six-aircraft team for the RNZAF 50th Anniversary celebrations in April 1987. This team performed with distinction at the 50th Anniversary of Christchurch International at Harewood in late March. Then followed two display days at RNZAF Ohakea and two more days at RNZAF Base Auckland.

The 1988 Australian Bicentennial Air Show, staged at RAAF Richmond, saw the Kiwi Red team steal the show with its exciting routine. Kiwi Red continued in 1989-90 for the opening of the Commonwealth Games under Wing Commander John Bates.

The national and international recognition of Number 75 Squadron as an aerobatic team flying Skyhawks was well established in the 1980s, restoring again the reputation begun with Vampires in the 1940s and maintained regularly in the 1964-70 period.

ARMÉE DE L'AIR FRANÇAISE
PATROUILLE DE FRANCE

The Patrouille de France (French Patrol) of the Armée de l'Air Française (French Air Force) is one of the world's oldest permanent military aerobatic teams, having been formed in 1953. It's first team, which was a direct ancestor of the Patrouille de France, the Patrouille d'Etampes was formed at Etampes in 1931, under the leadership of Captain Edouard Amouroux, and flew Morane 230s. Another team, the Patrouille Weiser, was formed at Dijon in 1934, but the Patrouille d'Etampes remained in place, moving to Salon-de-Provence in 1937, where it became the Armée de l'Air Flying School's *official* team.

Disbanded in 1939 because of World War II, the team reformed at Tours in 1946 as the Patrouille de Tours. The following year the team returned to Etampes and was designated as the official aerobatic team of the Armée de l'Air.

In the early 1950s, there was a proliferation of unofficial teams formed in Armée de l'Air squadrons using such jet fighters as de Havilland Vampires and Republic Thunder-

Right: Soaring high above the Arc de Triomphe, the French aerobatic team celebrates Bicentennial Day. *Below:* A rolling Alphajet. *Opposite top:* The Patrouille on patrol. *Opposite, bottom from left:* The dart and diamond eight-plane formations.

jets, and in 1953 the Patrouille de France was formed using Thunderjets. The American jets remained in service for one season before the Patrouille de France made the transition to French-built Dassault Ouragans in 1954.

For most of its first decade, the Patrouille de France was not a specific group of pilots or aircraft as was the case with the official teams of other nations, but rather, it was simply a designation assigned to various Armée de l'Air fighter squadrons on a rotating basis. These teams consisted of Dassault Ouragans until 1956, when Dassault Mystères were adopted.

In January 1964, the Patrouille de France was assigned as an entity to the Armée de l'Air Academy (formerly the Flying School) at Salon-de-Provence and re-equipped with Fouga Magister two-seat training aircraft, which were cheaper to operate than the Mystère fighters. The Magisters remained in service with the Patrouille de France until 16 September 1980, when they were retired after 810 performances, which had been viewed by an estimated 20 million people.

For the 1981 season, the Patrouille de France adopted the Alphajet, a twin-engine training/attack aircraft, which was developed jointly by Dassault-Breguet in France and Dornier in Germany. At the top of their loops, the Alphajets are flown six feet apart at 140 mph. Initiating their pull-outs, the aircraft fly at 400 mph. Their markings are predominantly blue with the white and red of the French tricolor added to the upper wing and tail surfaces.

Selected for an average three-year tour, the pilots, all officers and volunteers, have logged a minimum of 1500 hours of jet fighter aircraft flying time. Low altitude, tight formation flying demands discipline, concentration and practice. Two training flights are flown each day during the winter season, enabling the team to take part in numerous air shows in France and Europe, from April through October.

Each year a new show is prepared, based on a succession of various tight formations gracefully interconnected throughout the demonstration. The demonstration shows a great variety of inflight formations and bomb bursts. All the maneuvers are studied, and with exacting patience, flown, improved upon and finally perfected.

Above: **A Patrouille pair in vertical climb.** *Right:* **The Patrouille de France in diamond formation during their 7 May 1989 show at Cairo.**
Below from left: **Two soloists roll past one another over Abbotsford. A diamond formation goes over the top for the bomb burst maneuver. A break is performed, trailing tricolored smoke. The bomb burst concludes the 20 minute Patrouille de France show.**

KOMMANDO DER FLIEGERUND FLIEGERABWEHRTRUPPEN, SCHWEIZ
COMMANDEMENT DES TROUPES D'AVIATION ET DE DEFENSE CONTRE AVIONS, SUISSE
COMANDO DELLE TRUPPE D'AVIAZIONE E DI DIFESA CONTRAEREA, SUIZZERA

PATROUILLE SUISSE

As Colonel HR Haeberli of the Swiss Air Force puts it so succinctly, the Patrouille Suisse (Swiss Patrol), unlike the aerobatic teams of other air forces, is 'not regarded as a central element of the air force. For political reasons, that formation (though piloted by professionals) has an amateur status only.'

They are, however, the only European team that has, since the mid-1960s, used full-size strike aircraft rather than trainers or light attack aircraft. Equipped with four British- built Hunter aircraft, the Swiss Air Force display team appeared for the first time in 1964 under the name Patrouille Suisse at an exhibition held in Lausanne and later at the Fiftieth Jubilee of the Swiss Air Force in Dudendorf. As Colonel Haeberli recalls, 'It was never the intention to create a spectacle, but rather to demonstrate flying skills, teamwork, precision and the efficiency of Switzerland's Air Force.'

Having begun with four Hunters in 1964, the Patrouille Suisse added a fifth aircraft in 1970 and a sixth in 1978, enabling the team to perform impressive formations. The fifth and sixth team members brought variety into the display with solo performances, and today, the team consists of six pilots–one or two experienced reserve pilots and a chief trainer who directs the entire air display from the ground.

Knowing that an accident resulting from a display maneuver could jeopardize the very existence of the team, safety has always played an important role within Patrouille Suisse. For this reason, risky formations and head-on maneuvers have been deleted from the team's aerial displays and thus, accidents of the type that have occurred in other display teams have never affected Patrouille Suisse's program. The Swiss team has always 'placed its main emphasis on precision and exact formations, elegant change-overs from one formation into the

Below and opposite: **The Patrouille Suisse transition from six abreast to a six-plane wedge, then go over the top!**

Above: **The Patrouille Suisse over the alps.** *Right:* **Moving into an inverted dart formation.**

next and harmony throughout the whole aerial display program.'

The pilots who belong to the Patrouille Suisse are not engaged in aerobatics on a full-time, sanctioned basis, but volunteer to train in their free time. On an average of every three years, one to two pilots leave the team, usually to pursue careers with commercial airlines. However, there is always a large number of interested junior pilots. New candidates are not commandeered to join the team but are selected by a unanimous vote of the standing members. Good character, loyalty, comradeship and flying skill are prerequisites to join the team.

Having been accepted by the Patrouille Suisse, a new team member will undergo a special inaugural flight program, introducing him to the most demanding art of formation aerobatics. First, exercises flown will be to familiarize the pilot with flying in close formation with minimal separation between the aircraft of three to five feet. Initially, this is practiced in formations of only two aircraft. The training becomes progressively more difficult, advancing to vertical maneuvers and formation rolls. Eventually, the new pilot will be able to fly the whole display program with the rest of the team. The formations in the early stages are performed at high altitude, progressively lowering to the performance level of 300 feet. (The soloists fly even as low as 150 feet.) The displays are flown with speeds ranging from 200 to 500 mph, and acceleration forces of up to four to five Gs are encountered.

A new pilot will undergo up to 30 training flights before finally participating in an actual display program. Every display is filmed from the ground by video and after completion, the program will be discussed and reviewed with the chief trainer. Every year, three display programs are drawn up, suitable for different weather conditions and each lasting for about 16 minutes. For seven to eight months each year, however, the team trains on an average of only once a week.

At the International Air Tattoo held in England in 1979 with many display teams competing, the Patrouille Suisse was awarded the much-desired 'Shell Trophy.' Patrouille Suisse was also awarded the Ailes de Cristal trophy, which was presented by the Swiss Aviation journalists for the display team's achievements in Swiss aviation in 1982, and in 1988 the team received an honorary diploma for outstanding teamwork from the Fédération Aéronautique Internationale (FAI). In 1989, Patrouille Suisse received the Honorary Medal awarded at the AMEF 89 held in Dudendorf by the Swiss Pro Aero Foundation.

THE ROYAL AIR FORCE
THE RED ARROWS

Britain's Red Arrows were established in 1965 as their permanent RAF aerobatic team. Prior to that time, the RAF was represented in the aerobatic world by a succession of teams drawn from operational units. Probably the most notable were the Black Arrows, which were formed out of Number 111 Squadron in 1957. Originally composed of five all-black Hawker Hunters, the Black Arrows expanded to 22 aircraft in 1958. It was in this year at the Farnborough Air Show that the Black Arrows performed a 22-aircraft loop, constituting the largest formation of aircraft ever looped in a single maneuver.

The Black Arrows of Number 111 Squadron remained in service for four seasons and thereafter were replaced by a series of teams that changed annually for four years. In 1961, they were succeeded by the Blue Diamonds of Number 92 Squadron, and in turn by the Tigers of 74 Squadron in 1962 and by the Firebirds of Number 56 Squadron in 1963. The latter teams flew English Electric Lightnings, and as such were the last RAF aerobatic teams to fly first-line fighter aircraft.

In 1964, a decision having been made to use trainers rather than fighters for aerobatic displays, the RAF formed *two* aerobatic teams. These were the Yellowjacks of Number 4 Squadron, flying Hawker Siddley Gnats, and the Red Pelicans, flying BAC Jet Provost T4s. The Red Pelicans were formed at the Central Flying School, which at the time

was located at RAF Little Rissington in Gloucestershire. The aircraft of the two teams were prominently painted in the suggested colors.

Ironically, the Central Flying School had been the scene of the RAF's first organized aerobatic displays 40 years earlier when CFS pilots started putting on shows in de Havilland Genet Moths.

Following the 1964 season, the RAF decided to form a single team, although it was not until 1969 that it became officially 'permanent.' This team was formed using Gnats at the Central Flying School, under Flight Lieutenant Lee Jones, late of the Yellowjacks. The team, named Red Arrows, was initially based at RAF Fairford as a CFS detachment.

The new team practiced through the winter and had their debut at the Biggin Hill Air Fair in May 1965. This was in turn followed by some 50 appearances, including visits to Belgium, France, Italy, the Netherlands and West Germany. The Arrows were awarded the Britannia Trophy by the Royal Aero Club in recognition of their outstanding contribution to British prestige in the field of aviation.

In 1966, Squadron Leader Ray Hanna took over the seven-plane team and just under 90 shows were flown by

Below and opposite: **The nine ships of RAF's Red Arrows move into an eagle loop, which recovers as an apollo bend.**

Left: **A pair of Red Arrows, one of which is armed with air-to-air missiles.**
Above: **The seven-plane vixen break.**

the end of the 1966 season. Although technical problems with the Gnat necessitated a detailed structural check of each aircraft and delayed the start of the 1967 season, nearly 100 public appearances were made, nonetheless.

The following year, the RAF expanded its demonstration team from seven to nine pilots, and since that time (except in 1971 when they were a seven-plane team again) the Red Arrows 'Diamond Nine' formation has come to represent the peak of the RAF's precision formation flying. In 1969, based on public response to their demonstrations, the Red Arrows were designated as a permanent team and elevated to full squadron status within the RAF.

The Red Arrows gave 103 public performances in 1973, topping the century mark for the first time, and in 1977 they completed their 1000th show, for an average of 80 shows per year. The following two years, their last using the Gnat, the Red Arrows averaged 146 shows annually and visited 18 countries.

The Red Arrows first took delivery of their British Aerospace Hawks at the end of the 1979 season and made their debut in this new aircraft the next year. The Red Arrows have conducted ambitious world tours involving shows not only in Britain and Europe, but also in North America, the Middle East and Scandinavia. The most ambitious tour, to the Far East, was completed in 1986, involving 22 displays in 15 countries, and traveling 18,500 miles in six weeks. The Red Arrows had, by the end of the 1990 season, completed 2500 public displays, with the total number of countries visited totaling 38.

The annual display season typically begins in late spring, with each of the more than 100 Red Arrows events planned in detail for six weeks. This means that planning for more than one dozen events is usually at some stage of development at any given moment. For the three weeks prior to each event, the Red Arrows team manager and his staff maintain close contact with the event organizer, and a document is issued showing timings, transit routes, personnel involved and equipment required. On departure day, RAF Lockheed Hercules transport aircraft assigned to the Red Arrows arrives at their base at RAF Scampton and are loaded with spares, servicing equipment and first-line personnel not flying in the Red Arrows Hawks. In addition

to the Hercules, 10 Red Arrows Hawks, including one spare, are flown to the event airfield. The first-line engineering officer and nine technicians, called the 'Circus,' fly in the rear seats of the Hawks during transit flights, so that servicing can begin before the Hercules arrives.

Prior to each actual display, the pilots are briefed by the team leader on the prevailing weather, the display sequence, obstacles and any vital information relevant to the display site. The type of show depends on weather conditions, and there are three options: the full looping sequence in good weather and visibility; the rolling show in moderate weather, and the flat show in poor weather. These options are completely interchangeable, meaning that, if necessary, the display can change from 'full' to 'flat' and back to 'full' in two maneuvers if the weather is variable! The manager provides the commentary, while the photographer videotapes every maneuver, which is later studied and analyzed by the pilots at the end of each display debriefing. In the unlikely event that a pilot is unable to fly a display, the team has the option of flying a seven or eight aircraft show.

Three new pilots are added to the Red Arrows team at the end of the display season, and for a month they fly in the back seat behind an experienced pilot to get the feel for the team, the program and the required techniques. In early October as the season comes to a close, the new

Above: The Red Arrows' program begins with a big nine loop, followed by a big vixen roll that flows into the eagle loop seen here. *Right:* The Red Arrows are now well-known British landmarks. *Overleaf:* The Red Arrows in their characteristic diamond nine formation.

pilots practice looping and rolling in small formations, and, as proficiency grows, maneuvering altitude is lowered and the formations increase in size. A month later, the work-up has progressed to formations of seven aircraft, allowing servicing to be carried out on some of the airplanes, without any loss of value to the pilot practice time.

Through the off-season, the Red Arrows fly up to four sorties a day, with every practice being videotaped, with the tapes being analyzed and used for debriefings. Constant practice, discussion and changes, if needed, result in the display sequence being perfected. By January, all of the aircraft are available and the pilots are ready to fly nine aircraft formations. The winter work-up culminates with a detachment to Cyprus, where good flying weather guarantees continuity of flying and allows the final polish to be put on the display. The display sequence is then performed in front of the Commander-in-Chief of the RAF Support command, who must give his approval before the team can display before the public. When this is given, the Red Arrows are ready for another season of thrilling airshow audiences.

THE ROYAL NEW ZEALAND AIR FORCE

THE RED CHECKERS

Formation aerobatic teams have existed at the Central Flying School at Wigram near Christchurch since the 1940s, as aerobatics naturally provided an opportunity for flying instructors to both hone and demonstrate flying skills. These teams, flying North American Harvard trainers, existed informally until 1967, when the Red Checkers were officially formed.

The Red Checkers were extremely popular and performed throughout New Zealand until the energy crisis of 1973 forced the team to be disbanded in 1973.

In 1980, the Red Checkers were reformed using the New Zealand-built CT4 Airtrainer. While there is obvious political advantage to using the CT4, its 210 hp engine is much less powerful than the supercharged 550 hp radial on the old Harvard. This factor, however, lead to the Red Checkers being able to work much closer than a faster team such as Kiwi Red or the Blue Angels.

The Red Checkers show begins with a four-plane formation, plus a solo, with the two elements taking turns during the show, which includes aerobatics down to 500 feet and flybys at 100 feet.

All the team members are instructors at the Central Flying School and have an excellent safety record, with, as the CFS publicity department puts it, 'only a couple of minor touches to keep the boys on their toes.'

Below: **Members of the Royal New Zealand Air Force's Red Checkers Aerobatic Team flying the New Zealand built CT4 Airtrainer.** *Opposite:* **The Red Checkers flew the Harvard (T-6 Texan) until being disbanded in 1973.**

THE ROYAL AUSTRALIAN AIR FORCE
THE ROULETTES

The Roulettes of the Royal Australian Air Force made their first public appearance at RAAF Base Laverton on 21 August 1971, although the first RAAF aerobatic activity took place in 1934, also at Laverton. The first organized RAAF aerobatic team was the Meteorites of the Number 77 Squadron–flying Gloster Meteors—which were formed in 1958. This team was in turn succeeded by the Black Diamonds of the Number 75 Squadron that formed in 1961 with North American Sabre Jets produced under license in Australia by Commonwealth. Founded on the fortieth anniversary of the RAAF, the Black Diamonds survived for four air show seasons before being disbanded in 1964.

Meanwhile, Number 76 Squadron at Williamtown NSW formed two single season teams, the Black Panthers in 1962 and the Red Diamonds in 1963. Both of the Number 76 Squadron teams, like the Black Diamonds, used Sabres, and several Black Panther Sabres later were used by the Red Diamonds.

In September 1963, a year before the Black Diamonds disbanded, the Telstars were formed at the RAAF Central

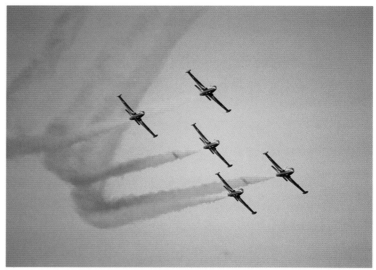

Above: The Roulettes swoop into the evening sky, smoke trails tinged by the evening sky. *Below:* Three Roulette Macchi jets in formation over the Victorian countryside. *Opposite:* The Roulettes overfly the Gippsland coast.

Left: **Over the top—the team in spectacular formation.** *Above:* **The Roulettes' amazing Mirror Pair go through their paces.**

Flying School, flying de Havilland Vampire trainers. The Telstars are noted as the direct predecessors of today's Roulettes. The next official RAAF aerobatic team was the Marksmen, formed in 1968 for a single season.

Also in 1968, the Telstars converted from Vampires to Aermacchi M3326Hs, designed in Italy but built in Australia by Commonwealth. Because of RAAF commitments to the war in Vietnam, the Telstars were briefly disbanded in 1968, and in 1971 they were renamed as the Roulettes.

In 1974, the Roulettes expanded to five, and then to seven, for the RAAF Diamond Jubilee in 1981. From 1982 to November 1988 the teams reverted to five Macchis, and from January to June 1989 a pair of Macchis performed a number of displays, as Central Flying School pilots gradually converted to the Swiss-designed Pilatus PC9/A.

In July 1989, the Central Flying School formed a team with PC9/A aircraft. Two aircraft were used until October 1989, after which the Roulettes expanded to five PC9/As. The team further expanded to six in January 1990, with their first display at Mt Gambier, South Australia, on 5 March 1990.

The PC9/A is a single-engined, low wing, tandem, two-seat aircraft used primarily as a trainer at Number 2 Flying Training School, RAAF Pearce, Western Australia, and at the Central Flying School, RAAF East Sale, Victoria. The PC9/A is powered by the Pratt & Whitney PT-7 turboprop, delivering 950 shaft horsepower. A feature of the aircraft is the ejection seat fitted to both cockpits which enables the pilot to abandon the aircraft in an emergency, such as engine failure at low level. The aircraft is manufactured under license in Australia by Hawker de Havilland.

Wherever the Roulettes travel away from their base at East Sale in Gippsland, Victoria, a small support team of engineers and technical personnel is deployed with them. These people assist in aircraft marshaling, refueling and replenishing engine oil and crew oxygen. The support team provides specialist support in rectifying any minor faults that may have occurred en route or during the display. Work conditions are often poor and work frequently has to be carried out quickly to ready the aircraft for the display.

All Roulette pilots are primarily instructors at the Central Flying School and volunteer their time to the team, unlike military formation aerobatic team members who have full-time professional status.

Above and opposite: Which way is up? The Mirror Pair (A23-002 and A23-005) in a remarkable aerial pas-de-deux over their base at East Sale Gippsland, Victoria.

The Roulettes adopted the Swiss-designed Pilatus PC9/A in 1989. It is interesting to note the number of countries whose official air force aerobatic teams are now using turboprop-powered aircraft rather than jets. Not only Australia, but Brazil as well, use turboprops primarily, while France and New Zealand have the Equipe de Voltige and Red Checkers as second-echelon aerobatic teams.

THE SOUTH AFRICAN AIR FORCE
THE SILVER FALCONS

Formed in November 1967, the Silver Falcons (Silber Valke in Afrikaans) were preceded by a team known as the Bumbling Bees. The former name was replaced because it had no easy bilingual translation, although in the 1980s, the Bumbling Bees were reactivated as a secondary SAAF aerobatic team.

The team was established under the direction of Commandant Chris Prins AFB Langebaanweg in the Western Cape, which is home to the 83d Flying School from which the volunteer pilots—all instructors at the school—are still drawn. Under the leadership of Colonel Prins (then a service test pilot), the four-man team laid the foundations for the traditionally tight, flowing displays for which the Falcons have become well known. The early 1970s saw a curb on flying due to world oil price hikes. However, from the mid-1970s to early 1980s the team went through another growth spurt, confirming the reputation already set, with memorable displays at the Lanseria Airshows.

The aircraft acquired the first phase of their present striking color scheme under Commandant John Rankin in 1985, and since then things have gone from strength to strength. Under Commandant Dave Knoesen, the aircraft acquired the second phase of development, and the paint scheme with colorful under surfaces.

By the mid-1980s, the frequency of the Silver Falcons' shows doubled to an average of 15 shows per season (February to October), and an extra member was introduced in the form of a Synchro Soloist in 1988. This addition introduced a flexibility factor and improved entertainment value—this at a time when the South African air show circuit included the very polished Winfield Magnum Pitts Team (led by Scully Levin, a South African Airways 747 Captain and ex-SAAF pilot). Commentary for the shows is done by Brian Emmenis, a popular South African radio personality. His infectious enthusiasm, together with his aptly chosen music, has greatly enhanced the quality of the shows. To insure that interest in the team is satisfied, the 'Friends of the SAAF Museum' maintains stands at air shows to sell posters, stickers and brochures.

In addition to its 15 shows in South Africa each year, the team performs all over the world, from Japan to Finland, Brazil and Canada, and has suffered no fatal accidents and only one aircraft loss (due to engine fire) in 21 years. The Silver Falcons have much of which to be proud.

The team flies the Atlas Impala, the South African-built version of the Italian-designed Aermacchi MB326M. The Impala Mk I is powered by a Rolls Royce Viper engine and was selected for its good control balance in the required speed range. The aircraft's two main drawbacks, from the standpoint of the SAAF, are its limited power and lack of powered controls. The former is ever present for line-astern members, and is aggravated particularly when per-

forming at altitudes of 5000 to 6000 feet, with density altitudes in the order of 9000 feet. In combination with the lack of power, the lack of powered controls thus restricts the team from flying as a bigger team and from introducing more spectacular maneuvers. Thus, taking note of these realities and because of its part-time nature the team prefers to stay within its limitations.

Apart from carrying a diesel tank in the rear cockpit to produce smoke, the only other modification that distinguishes the aircraft from the other line aircraft is the color scheme, which was developed between 1987 and 1989 for the Silver Falcons. It started by introducing a very effective coloring of the fuselage, tail and tip tanks in the national colors (orange, white and blue). The second and final development was to paint (in the same colors) a triangular arrow on the underside of the wing surfaces. This is very similar to the livery of the Frecci Tricolori team.

Silver Falcon pilots are all experienced flying instructors from the 83d Flying School, based at Langebaanweg. They are volunteers and practice in their spare time, with the Commanding Officer of the Flying School leading the team. The fact that the team practices outside of working hours, distinguishes it from British or American military jet teams, which are full-time teams. New members receive about 20 hours of practice before their first display and will take over whichever slot becomes vacant. The numbers of the team members do not reflect any particular seniority, excluding the leader, of course.

The display sequence includes about 10 different maneuvers and lasts between 12 and 15 minutes, depending on altitude. A bad weather display sequence of fewer maneuvers can also be given. All the maneuvers are common to formation aerobatics.

Spectacular formation changes are generally a rare feature of the sequences, partly because of the limitations described above, as well as the limitations imposed by the aircraft. Generally, the formation changes are hidden, with the aim being subtlety. However, some changes are carried out in full view of the crowd if there is much visual impact to be gained. One such change was flown by the 1983 team. The sequence started with a four-ship line abreast loop coming from behind the crowd. The aircraft remained in line abreast until just past the apex, when, on a command, they rolled simultaneously through 90 degrees into a four-ship line astern formation. Thus, a breath-taking formation change was affected with a 'very neat change in direction.'

Above and opposite: **The Silver Falcons over the veldt in their Atlas Impalas. The Impala is a South African version of the Italian Aermacchi MB326M.** *Below:* **North American Harvard number 7688 from the Central Flying School at Dunnottar, piloted by Major Ray Houghton. The Harvard, originally designed in the 1930s, is still used as a trainer by the SAAF and by the Bumbling Bees aerobatic team. The Bee team was reactivated during the 1980s.**

THE CANADIAN ARMED FORCES/
FORCES ARMÉES CANADIENNES
THE SNOWBIRDS

Founded in 1971 at Canadian Forces Base Moose Jaw in Saskatchewan, the Snowbirds trace their heritage to the Golden Centennaires, a team formed in 1967 to help celebrate the 100th anniversary of the Dominion of Canada. The Golden Centennaires flew six gold and black Canadair CL-41 Tutors (plus two spares and a pair of T-33 Silver Stars as support aircraft), and were led by Wing Commander OB Philp in 100 performances beginning and ending at Expo 67 in Montreal. The Royal Canadian Air Force (now Canadian Armed Forces) disbanded the Golden Centennaires in October 1967, but Wing Commander (later Colonel) Philp maintained the idea of a permanent Canadian aerobatic team, and four years later, he was instrumental in establishing the Snowbirds.

The aerobatic tradition in the RCAF dates to the formation of the Siskins in 1929. Flying the Armstrong Whitworth aircraft of the same name, the Siskins performed at 55 airshows in Canada and the United States until they were disbanded at the end of the 1931 season.

Although the RCAF continued to give aerobatic displays, the next organized team did not appear until well after World War II. These were the Blue Devils, formed by RCAF 410 Squadron at St Hubert, Quebec in 1949. Despite its name, the team's de Havilland Vampires carried a natural metal finish. In 1950, the Blue Devils took on members of 421 Squadron and were known formally as the Air Defence Group Aerobatic Team. Despite this official imprimatur and a full series of popular appearances in Canada and the United States, the Blue Devils were disbanded at the end of September 1950.

It would be 1959 before the RCAF again had a formal aerobatic team. In the interim, however, several single-season teams were formed for regional exhibitions. In 1954, two teams were created–the Pacific Prairie Team, out of Cold Lake, Alberta, and the Fireballs, which was formed in Soellingen, West Germany from RCAF squadrons assigned to NATO in Europe. The former performed throughout Canada's western and prairie provinces, while the latter represented Canada at European airshows.

In 1955, the Fireballs team was succeeded by the Sky Lancers, formed from the RCAF's Second Fighter Wing stationed at Grosentiquin in France. While the Canadair Sabres of the Fireballs had been painted bright red overall, the Sky Lancers retained the camouflage colors on their Sabres.

In 1959, the Golden Hawks were formed at Trenton, Ontario to help celebrate 50 years of flight in Canada and the 35th anniversary of the RCAF itself. Flying Canadair

Above and opposite: **The Snowbird's nine-plane big diamond over Abbotsford in 1987, compared to the smaller, but no less spectacular, seven-plane double diamond.**

Sabres, the Golden Hawks flew 65 airshows in their first season and remained in service until February 1964, by which time they had given 317 public performances over five seasons. Also in 1959, a team called the Gimli Smokers was formed at Downsview, Ontario. Flying Canadair Silver Stars, they performed for only a single season.

Meanwhile, at the RCAF's Portage La Prairie training base, a unique concept in military aerobatic teams came to pass. It was, in fact, not a team at all, but a solo, all-red Silver Star called the Red Knight, and the concept survived for an entire decade. There were 11 Red Knights, including

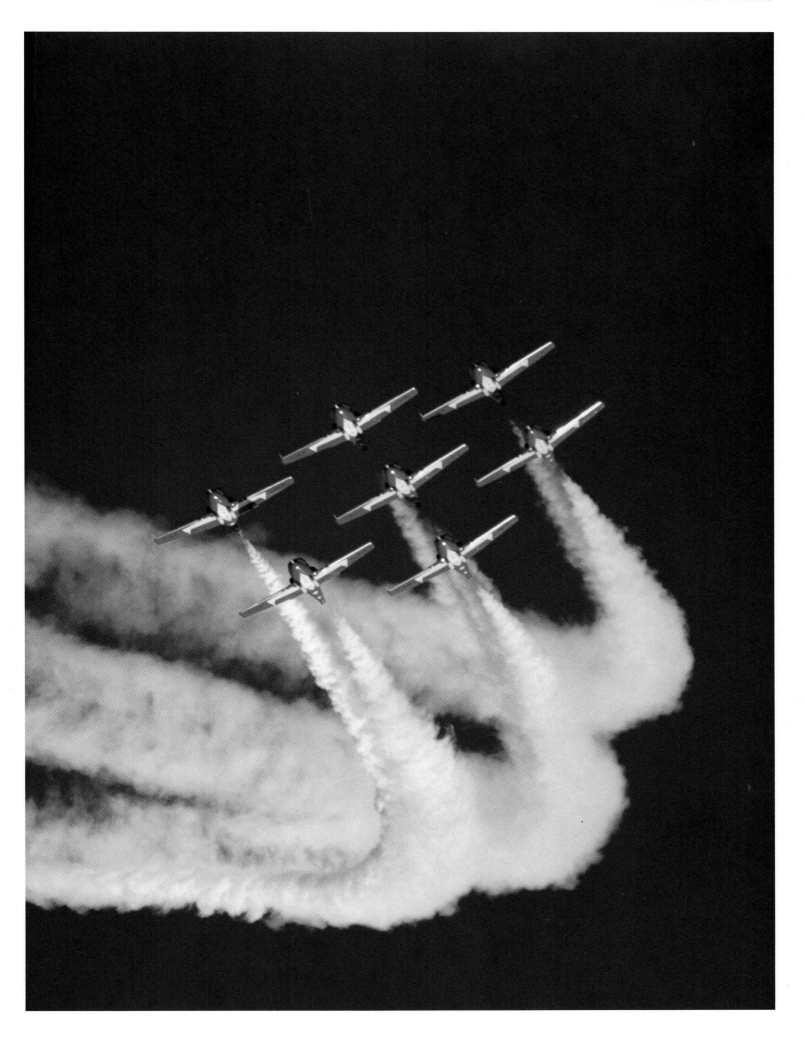

Roy Windover (1959), Bob Hallowell (1960), Dave Barker (1961-62), Bill Frazer (1963), Bud Morin (1963), Wayne McLellan (1964), Tex Deagnon (1965), Terry Hallett (1966), Jack Waters (1967) Dave Curran (1968) and Bryan Alston (1969). The series of Canadair Silver Stars used by the Red Knights was abandoned in 1968 in favor of a Canadair Tutor, the type of aircraft still used by today's Snowbirds.

In 1962, an unofficial and controversial team was formed at the RCAF's Moose Jaw base. Called Goldilocks, they were essentially a tongue-in-cheek parody of the Golden Hawks, consisting of seven yellow and red World War II-era North American Harvard trainers. A flamboyant team, they were very popular with audiences, and as this popularity grew, they became somewhat of an embarrassment to RCAF headquarters, which eventually ordered this parody disbanded at the end of the 1963 season.

The Golden Centennaires of 1967 planted the seed which ultimately led to the creation of the Snowbirds. Colonel OB Philp, the Commanding Officer of the Centennaires, became the Base Commander of CFB Moose Jaw, but he never forgot his team of 1967. He wanted to ensure that the traditions of aerial perfection established by teams such as the Golden Hawks and his own Golden Centennaires would not be lost, so he established an unofficial, non-aerobatic formation team at Moose Jaw in 1971. The team was made up of volunteer instructor pilots, and operations were conducted on a local, base level as the Second Canadian Forces Formation Team Squadron (2CFFTS). Seven ex-Centennaire Tutors, which had already been repainted white, were utilized, as they were readily distinguishable from the other natural metal aircraft of the Moose Jaw fleet. The 2CFFTS team members practiced in

the evenings after completing their primary instructional duties, and performed on weekends. The new team was named Snowbirds as a result of a contest held at the base elementary school, and first flew under this name at the 1971 Saskatchewan Homecoming Airshow on 11 July. This performance was followed by appearances at other major airshows, such as Abbotsford, and at military bases across Canada. During the show season, which lasted from June to the end of August, the team performed 27 shows. Public response indicated that the reforming of a Canadian formation team was a popular move.

In 1972, two solo aircraft were added to the formation, and the practice of holding a flying competition to choose the pilots for the team was introduced; nine pilots were chosen from the school following the competition in February of that year. The selected air crew and ground crew worked on the team on a full-time basis for the duration of the show season. From May to September, the team performed 25 shows, and for the first time visited the northern communities of Fort Smith and Yellowknife.

In 1973, the show was expanded to include aerobatic formation maneuvers, but formation changes during these maneuvers were still prohibited. The show season began in May with what was to become the annual 'Northern Tour,' followed by shows across Canada and the United States. At this time, funding for the team still came from the base budget and Training Command.

In 1974, for the first time, the try-out competition was opened to pilots from bases throughout the Canadian

Below: Slaunched and dished, three Snowbirds make a low pass. *Right:* The Snowbirds bank gracefully in concorde formation

Forces. The team was cleared to perform a fully aerobatic formation display, and the distinctive red, white and blue paint scheme, that still exists, was adopted. The team deployed to CFB Comox in April for a work-up period designed to test deployment procedures and expose team members to new show sites with difficult terrain features. This spring training session at Comox has become an annual operation. During the Northern tour that year, with a performance at Inuvik, the Snowbirds became the first North American formation team to fly a show north of the Arctic Circle. At the end of the season, the team had flown 80 shows, with an estimated viewing audience of two million people.

In 1975, the Snowbirds were made a separate but still not permanent unit of the Canadian Forces, integral to CFB Moose Jaw under Air Command. One of the highlights of the 70-show 1975 season was a *midnight* performance on 11 May at Inuvik in the 'land of the midnight sun.'

In 1976, the growing popularity of the team in the United States was reflected in the request for a performance at a show at Philadelphia on the 4th of July as part of the American Bicentennial celebration. In Canada, the team performed at both Montreal and Kingston as part of the ceremonies during the 1976 Summer Olympics in Montreal.

In September 1977, the Snowbirds were finally made a permanent unit, and their official designation became the Canadian Forces Air Demonstration Team (CFADT). On 1 April 1978, the CFADT received squadron status, and the Snowbirds became 431 (Air Demonstration) Squadron. 431 'Iroquois' Squadron, *The Hatiten Ronteriios* or 'Warriors of the Air,' had been a World War II bomber squadron that was disbanded in 1945. It was reformed briefly in 1954 as an F-86 Sabre squadron, which contributed four aircraft to the Prairie Pacific aerobatic teams.

During the 1979 and 1980 seasons, the Snowbirds' performance featured an expanded opening nine-plane sequence that received popular acclaim with an estimated audience throughout North America of over five million spectators. In 1981, for the first time, the show opened and closed with nine-plane formation sequences, and this was performed in 1982 before a total audience of more than six million fans. In 1984, the team helped celebrate the 75th anniversary of powered flight in Canada and the 60th anniversary of the Royal Canadian Air Force. In 1986, several performances were flown over the Expo '86 site in Vancouver, with the Snowbirds as one of five jet demonstration teams gathered from around the world to perform at the Abbotsford International Airshow on 9 August 1986. Highlighting the 1988 season were the opening ceremonies of the Winter Olympic Games in Calgary, Alberta, where the team's performance was witnessed by almost two billion people around the world.

The year 1990 represented the 20th anniversary season of the Canadian Forces Snowbirds, again with Major Dempsey leading the team. The season featured 74 displays in 53 locations, with performances from Gander, Newfoundland to El Paso, Texas. Early in the 1990 season, the Snowbirds performed their 1000th official air demonstration.

Below: **Leaving a sleek trail of smoke behind them, the Snowbirds perform an inverted big arrow formation.** *Right:* **In precise unison, a concorde of Snowbirds elegantly completes a loop above Canadian Forces Base at Bagotville, Quebec.**

THE UNITED STATES AIR FORCE
THE THUNDERBIRDS

The Thunderbirds were established on 1 June 1953 as the 3600th Air Demonstration Squadron of the US Air Force Tactical Air Command. Originally based at Luke AFB near Phoenix, Arizona, the 3600th is now based at Nellis AFB near Las Vegas, Nevada.

The 3600th first took the name Stardusters, but it was soon changed to Thunderbirds, influenced to a large degree by the strong regional Indian culture and folklore of the Southwestern United States, where Luke AFB is located.

In North American Indian lore, the Thunderbird was believed to control nearly all powers man could imagine, especially the invincible forces of good conquering evil and light overcoming dark. Indian tribes from Mexico to as far north as Alaska knew of the mythical deity who alone could grant success in war. They believed the being commanded the elements, willing the lightning and thunder to flash and crackle in the sky in an awesome display of light and sound. They also believed it caused rain to fall upon the earth. The Indians envisioned the Thunderbird as a huge creature of the sky, with features resembling those of both the hawk and the eagle. The sky was its kingdom, and from there it ruled over its domain. Lightning flashed from its eyes and thunder rolled from its wings.

Based on prototypical images from the pottery of the Zuni tribe, the emblem for the newly-formed team was designed by First Lieutenant Bob 'Mac' McCormick, the team's first solo pilot. The choice of colors—red, white and blue—not only coincide with the Indians' vision of the Thunderbird, but also represent the colors of the American flag. The Thunderbirds today are the living legend of the great beast of Indian folklore—the roar and fire of their sleek F-16 Fighting Falcons are like thunder and lightning.

The purpose of the Thunderbirds was, and is today, to plan and present precision aerial maneuvers demonstrating the capabilities of modern Air Force jet aircraft and the exacting professional skills the service develops in its people to fly and maintain these aircraft. Along with this mission, the Thunderbirds have been used to 'support Air Force recruiting and retention programs, and to reinforce public confidence in the US Air Force.' Additional objectives include supporting Air Force relations and people-to-people programs. The squadron also maintains the capability of rapid integration into a combat role, if required.

Just seven days after the Thunderbirds were officially formed in 1953, the team performed its first aerial show for its home base. Since then, the Thunderbirds have dis-

Right: The US Air Force's Thunderbirds demonstration team adopted the image of a powerful American Indian deity as their trademark. *Top right:* Smoke billowing, the Thunderirds soar through their maneuvers.

played their aerial artistry for millions of spectators in 52 countries worldwide.

When the team was first established, they selected the Republic F-84G Thunderjet. It had a maximum speed of 600 mph and had been used extensively as a fighter-bomber in the Korean conflict. During the F-84G years, the Thunderbirds had a highly successful tour of major South American capitals, and later toured Central American nations as well. In early 1955, the Thunderbirds transitioned for a year to the swept-wing F-84F Thunderstreak. During its first three years, the team performed 222 shows before more than nine million spectators in the Republic F-84s.

In 1956, the Thunderbirds adopted the world's first supersonic jet fighter, the North American F-100 Super Sabre, an aircraft that was to be their aerial platform for 14 years. This was also the year the Thunderbirds left their nest at Luke AFB and moved to their present home at Nellis AFB. The F-100 years were memorable. Millions of people in the United States, South and Central America, Europe and the Caribbean countries, North Africa, Turkey and the Far East marveled at the Thunderbirds' artistry and precision.

During November and December 1959, the team traded its F-100Cs for F-100Ds for 31 shows during a Far East tour covering Taiwan, Korea, Japan, Okinawa, the Philippines and Hawaii. This temporary transition was necessary because of the F-100C's inability to air refuel during the vast distances that had to be covered. More than three million people watched the team in this impressive example of rapid airpower deployment, which logged more than 24,000 air miles. For this tour, the Thunderbirds received Air Force aviation's highest honor, the 1959 MacKay Trophy, for making 'the most meritorious flight of the year.'

The team briefly used the Republic F-105 Thunderchief for a part of the 1964 air demonstration season. However, after only six shows, the Thunderbirds returned to the F-100D due to an extensive modification that became necessary on all US Air Force F-105 aircraft.

In 1965, the Thunderbirds flew an all-time high of 121 aerial demonstrations, including their 1000th performance, flown before 25,000 spectators at Waukegan, Illinois. Overseas tours that year included the Caribbean, Europe and Latin America, covering a total of 23 countries. The last F-100 performance came at Nellis AFB on 30 November 1968. In all, the Thunderbirds flew 1111 air demonstrations using the Super Sabre.

In 1969, the Thunderbirds switched to the McDonnell Douglas F-4E Phantom II, an aircraft that at the time was the leading air superiority fighter in the US Air Force, and, indeed, worldwide. It is worth noting that the US Navy's Blue Angels also transitioned to F-4 Phantom IIs for their 1969 airshow season. The first show in the new aircraft was performed before President Richard Nixon on 4 June 1969 at the US Air Force Academy near Colorado Springs.

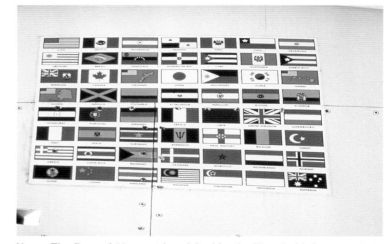

Above: The flags of 53 countries visited by the Thunderbirds grace their F-16 fuselages. *Below:* The Thunderbirds used the North American F-100 Super Sabre for a dozen years between 1956 and 1968.

The entire aerial demonstration was telecast nationally and viewed by millions. The following year, the Thunderbirds performed 106 F-4E air demonstrations while traveling 96,784 air miles to 30 states, Canada, Venezuela, Puerto Rico, Panama and the Bahamas. In 1971, the Thunderbirds again thrilled millions of Europeans during a 30-day tour that included stops in Spain, France, Denmark, Germany, Belgium, Italy and Morocco. Attendance for the year was nearly seven million, with the largest show audience at Le Bourget Airport, Paris, France—800,000 the first day and 1,500,000 on the second.

The Thunderbirds completed their 21st year of aerial demonstrations and their last show in the F-4E on 10 November 1973 at New Orleans. The F-4Es had flown a total of 518 shows and, in 1973 alone, the Thunderbirds performed before more than 12 million spectators in the United States and Latin America—then a record for a single year's attendance.

Above: The Thunderbirds' 1990 team members—the Air Forces' 'Ambassadors in Blue'—pose with an F-16. *Below:* The Northrop T-38 Talon was used by the team from 1974 through 1982.

In 1974, the Thunderbirds selected Northrop's T-38A Talon, the world's first supersonic trainer. Although the Talon was not in the Thunderbird tradition of using combat fighters, it did meet the objective of demonstrating the capabilities of notable Air Force aircraft. It was also more fuel-efficient and less expensive to maintain than a first-line combat aircraft. The worldwide energy crisis of 1974, which played a role in the Air Force's decision to trade down from the F-4E, also led to the Thunderbirds' shortest season on record: just 35 shows in four months.

America's Bicentennial, 1976, found the Thunderbirds performing a flyover at the opening of the National Air & Space Museum in Washington, DC. During the eight years they flew T-38s, they performed 598 official demonstrations in 47 states, Canada, Puerto Rico and the Dominican Republic.

In 1983, the Thunderbirds resumed an earlier tradition by adopting the Air Force's newest front-line fighter, the General Dynamics F-16 Fighting Falcon. During that same year, more than 16 million people in 33 states watched the team perform its aerial artistry. Aside from the aerial demonstrations, more than 115,000 people attended 245 Thunderbirds public relations events.

In 1984, following a 13-year absence, the Thunderbirds returned to Europe, where more than three million people in 11 countries attended their aerial shows. During this tour, the Thunderbirds visited Norway for the first time.

The second overseas deployment for the red, white and blue F-16s involved a 1985 tour of Latin America. During visits to four countries in 11 days, crowds of one million were recorded at Quito, Ecuador and Brazilia, Brazil. In all, 75 air demonstrations were flown in 1985, with more than 14 million people in attendance. By the close of the 1986 season, the Thunderbirds had performed a total of 296 air demonstrations for more than 48 million people.

In 1987, the Thunderbirds flew to the Far East for the first time since 1959. The Air Force's 'Ambassadors in Blue'

performed in eight countries, Guam and Hawaii. The team completed 15 airshows in 35 days for nearly two million spectators. The year 1987 will also be remembered for the Thunderbirds' debut visit to Beijing, China. The summer of 1987 also saw the team's record-breaking single day crowd count, when on 4 July, 2,250,000 people viewed a demonstration at Coney Island, New York.

The Thunderbirds are a six-plane team consisting of a leader, left wing, right wing, slot position, lead solo and opposing solo. A seventh and eighth F-16 are flown by the logistics officer and advanced coordinator. The remainder of the 3600th is composed of nearly 130 highly-skilled technicians in aircraft maintenance, public affairs, operations, supply, life support, communications, administration, photography and graphics. It's their job to ensure that the planes are ready for each demonstration and the myriad of small details inherent to every performance are complete.

Six of the flyers in the squadron are demonstration pilots, two are support officers and there is one logistics officer and a narrator. The latter two positions call for qualified tactical pilots who apply flying skills to each demonstration, media orientation flights and other responsibilities. Executive and maintenance duties are performed by the squadron's support officers. When a vacancy occurs, a thorough screening of applicants is made, with particular emphasis on the pilot's performance

Below: The Thunderbirds execute a perfect vertical climb and a two-plane breakaway. *Right:* The Thunderbirds streak across the heavens in a four-plane diamond formation.

record, appearance and written recommendations. In the pilot selection process, an applicant must have at least 1000 flying hours in a high performance jet aircraft prior to applying. Background and experience are closely scrutinized by current team members.

Several semifinalists normally accompany the team on actual demonstration deployments during the selection process. This travel allows potential Thunderbird officers to experience travel conditions and demands that go along with the job. It also gives team members a chance to personally observe each applicant's skills and attitudes. As the field is narrowed, applicants travel to Nellis AFB for extensive personal interviews and thorough medical evaluations. Demonstration pilot applicants are further tested during actual formation flying.

Once the commander/leader makes his decision, a Thunderbirds enlisted member begins a 21-day training and orientation period within the squadron. Thunderbird officers serve a two-year tour, but only one-half of the demonstration pilots rotate each year, providing a smooth transition for training newly-assigned pilots.

The annual Thunderbirds program now begins in March, ends in mid-November and includes about 100 flying demonstrations, with the peak months of June through August averaging about 15 shows each. In addition to major overseas tours (which are not conducted every year), the Thunderbirds make appearances throughout the United States and Canada, with nearly half of the shows being in conjunction with open houses at air force bases.

Left: **The Thunderbirds' Mirror Pair in level flight.** *Below:* **Performed at high speeds, the breathtaking two-plane crossover has dazzled crowds around the world.**

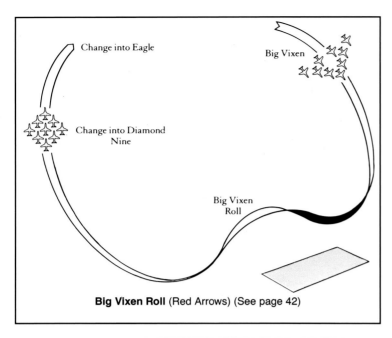

Big Vixen Roll (Red Arrows) (See page 42)

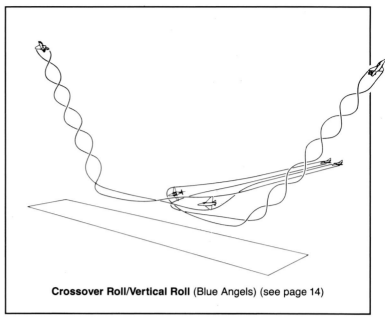

Crossover Roll/Vertical Roll (Blue Angels) (see page 14)

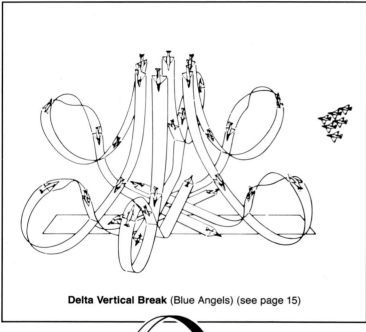

Delta Vertical Break (Blue Angels) (see page 15)

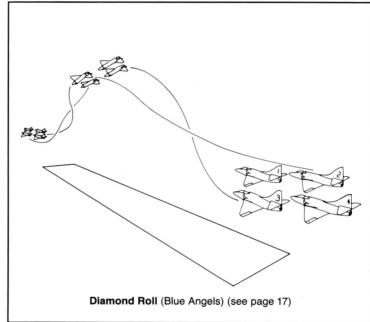

Diamond Roll (Blue Angels) (see page 17)

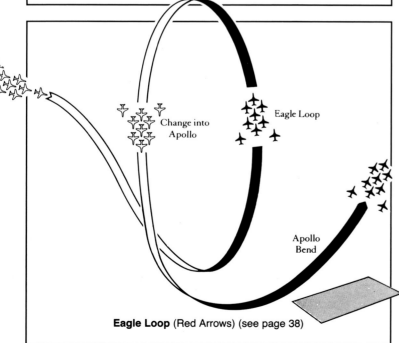

Eagle Loop (Red Arrows) (see page 38)

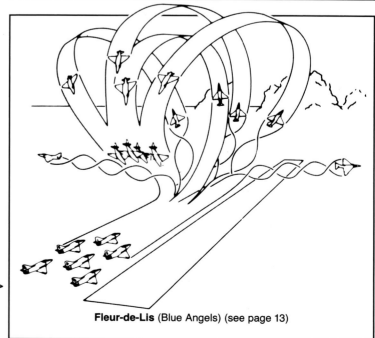

Fleur-de-Lis (Blue Angels) (see page 13)

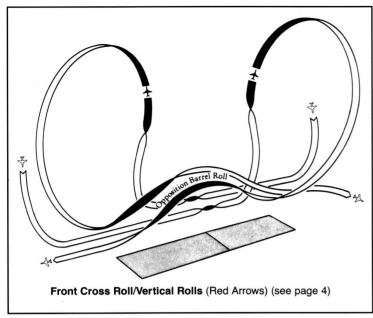

Front Cross Roll/Vertical Rolls (Red Arrows) (see page 4)

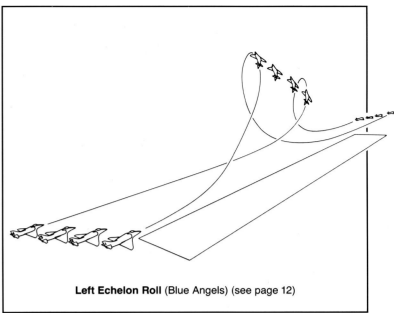

Left Echelon Roll (Blue Angels) (see page 12)

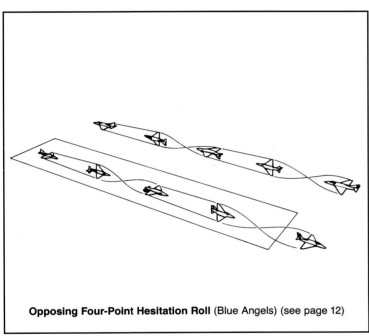

Opposing Four-Point Hesitation Roll (Blue Angels) (see page 12)

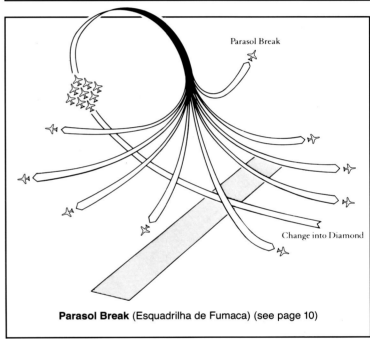

Parasol Break (Esquadrilha de Fumaca) (see page 10)

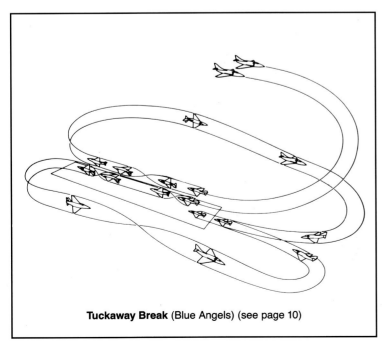

Tuckaway Break (Blue Angels) (see page 10)

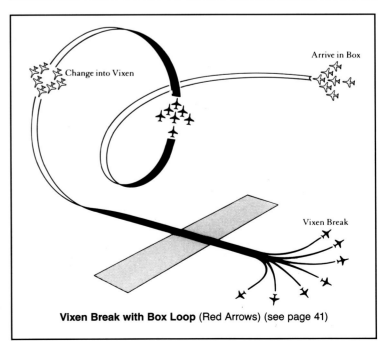

Vixen Break with Box Loop (Red Arrows) (see page 41)

THE AEROBATS

INDEX

Right: An Aermacchi MB326H of the Royal Australian Air Force Roulettes team.

Gatefold, outside: The US Navy's Blue Angels on their breathtaking diamond roll formation.

Gatefold, inside: Wingtip to wingtip with gear down, US Navy Blue Angels F/A-18 Hornets plummet toward San Francisco Bay. In the Blue Angels' repertoire, both the delta vertical break and fleur-de-lis feature multiplane 'nose dives.'

The Blue Angels' annual Fleet Week show held each October in San Francisco is one of the Bay Area's most popular events, typically garnering an audience of a million people.

Back page: The Red Arrows in the nine-plane formation from which they enter their delta roll maneuver.